Luka Houghton

Windows 11

Made simple for you

Contents

Disclaimer

The information provided in this book is for informational purposes only. The author makes no representations or warranties, express or implied, as to the completeness, accuracy, reliability, suitability, or availability of the contents of this book. Any reliance you place on such information is therefore strictly at your own risk.

Automated technologies may have been involved in the creation and/or translation of the content of this book. In no event will the author be liable for any loss or damage, including without limitation, indirect or consequential loss or damage, or any loss or damage whatsoever arising from loss of data or profits arising from , or in connection with, the direct and/or indirect use of this book.

If the reader does not partially or fully accept this disclaimer, he or she should refrain from using the contents of this book in any manner and should immediately delete or destroy the book.

Introduction

Whether you're new to Windows or migrating from a previous version, this book is designed to guide you step-by-step through the many features and improvements of Windows 11.

With its modern interface and new features, Windows 11 delivers an enriched user experience, while maintaining the familiarity that Windows users have enjoyed for years. This handy guide was created to help you quickly and efficiently master this operating system, whether navigating menus, customizing your workspace, or taking advantage of advanced productivity tools.

Each chapter in this book is carefully structured to meet your specific needs, from initial Windows 11 setup to advanced file management and troubleshooting tips. You'll also learn how to optimize your system's security, take advantage of backup and recovery features, and much more.

Whether you want to learn what's new in Windows 11, improve your productivity, or simply get familiar with this modern operating system, this guide is your ideal companion. Get ready to explore Windows 11 and discover everything it has to offer to make your computing experience smoother and more enjoyable.

We invite you to dive into this book and make Windows 11 your everyday digital ally.

Configuration and Installation of Windows 11

System requirements for Windows 11

System requirements for Windows 11 represent a set of technical specifications that determine the compatibility and optimal performance of the operating system on a computer. Microsoft has introduced stricter criteria compared to previous versions, aimed at improving security, reliability and functionality of the user experience. To install and run Windows 11, there are several key hardware components to consider.

First of all, the processor is a crucial element. Windows 11 requires at least a 64-bit processor with at least 1 GHz clock frequency, supporting an SSE2, PAE and NX instruction set. For example, Intel processors 8th generation (Coffee Lake) or newer, as well as AMD Ryzen 2000 series processors or newer, generally meet the minimum Windows 11 requirements.

RAM is also a determining factor. Microsoft recommends at least 4 GB of RAM for standard Windows 11 use, although for optimal performance, especially when multitasking and with memory-intensive applications, a higher capacity is preferable. For example, 8 GB of RAM is often recommended for a smooth and responsive user experience.

Internal storage is another important criterion. Windows 11 requires at least 64 GB of available storage space for the basic installation of the operating system. However, it is advisable to have more storage space for updates, applications and personal files. SSDs are particularly recommended for increased performance compared to traditional hard drives.

As for the graphics card, Windows 11 requires support for DirectX 12 and WDDM 2.x to benefit from all the advanced visual and graphics features of the operating system. This includes support for GPU-accelerated DirectX Raytracing (DXR) for games and applications using this technology.

Another aspect to consider is the TPM (Trusted Platform Module). Windows 11 requires support for TPM version 2.0, which helps strengthen the security of the operating system by enabling boot integrity verification and other advanced security features. Most modern computers, especially those produced after 2016, include TPM 2.0, but some users may need to enable this feature in their system's BIOS.

Additionally, compatibility with UEFI (Unified Extensible Firmware Interface) is required for installing Windows 11. UEFI is gradually replacing the traditional BIOS by providing advanced boot and security features. Most computers manufactured in recent years support UEFI, but the firmware configuration should be checked to ensure compatibility with Windows 11.

Finally, internet connectivity is important for installing updates and accessing some cloud-based features of Windows 11. Although not essential for the initial installation of the operating system, a stable and fast internet connection is recommended for Take full advantage of Microsoft online services and features.

How to install Windows 11 on your PC

Installing Windows 11 on a PC requires a methodical approach to ensure smooth integration and proper configuration of the operating system. Before starting the installation process, it is crucial to check your PC's hardware compatibility with the minimum Windows 11 requirements, such as CPU, RAM, storage, and other key components. Make sure your PC meets the required criteria to avoid potential problems during and after installation.

Once you have confirmed hardware compatibility, the next step is to backup all your important data. Although installing Windows 11 does not necessarily require deleting your personal files, it is still recommended to backup your data to an external device or the cloud to avoid accidental loss.

The Windows 11 installation process can be done from a bootable USB drive or installation DVD. You can create a bootable USB drive by downloading Microsoft's Media Creation Tool and following the instructions provided to copy the Windows 11 installation files to the USB drive. Make sure the USB drive has sufficient capacity and is configured to boot your PC from USB in BIOS or UEFI.

Once the USB drive is prepared, restart your PC and boot from the USB drive. You will be guided through the Windows 11 setup wizard, where you will need to select the language, time format, and keyboard preferences. Next, click "Install Now" to start the actual installation process.

During installation, you will be prompted to enter the Windows 11 product key if you have one, although this step can be bypassed if your PC has already been pre-activated with a digital license for Windows 10 or Windows 11. Follow the on-screen instructions to choose which edition of Windows 11 you want to install (for example, Windows 11 Home or Windows 11 Pro).

Next, you will need to select the location where you want to install Windows 11. You can create new partitions or use existing partitions on your hard drive or SSD. It is recommended to select a partition with enough free space for installation and for future operating system updates.

Once you have selected the installation location, follow the on-screen instructions to complete the installation process. Windows 11 will copy the necessary files, install features and updates, and perform initial system setup. The computer may restart several times during this process, which is normal.

Once the installation is complete, you will be prompted to configure basic Windows 11 settings, such as Internet connection, user account, and privacy settings. Once these steps are finalized, you will be welcomed to the Windows 11 desktop, ready to start exploring and using your new operating system. Be sure to check for available updates through Windows Update to ensure your system is secure and up to date.

Windows 11 User Interface

Discovering the new Start menu

The discovery of the new Start menu in Windows 11 represents a significant evolution compared to previous versions of Microsoft's operating system. This menu has been completely redesigned to provide a more intuitive user experience focused on the needs of modern users. Unlike the live tiles used in Windows 10, the Windows 11 Start menu takes a simplified approach with a layout focused on recent apps and documents. This new organization aims to facilitate quick access to frequently used applications and recent files, thereby reducing the time needed to start tasks.

Pinned apps take center stage in the new Start menu. Users can pin their favorite apps directly to the dedicated section, allowing instant access without having to navigate through multiple menus or search for shortcuts scattered across the desktop. For example, by clicking on a pinned app like Microsoft Edge or Microsoft Word, users can launch the app directly from the Start menu, simplifying daily app management.

In addition to pinned applications, the Windows 11 Start menu includes a dynamic list of recent documents. This feature allows users to easily pick up where they left off, displaying recently opened files in various applications. For example, a user could quickly find a Word document they were recently working on, without having to navigate through folders or launch the application from scratch.

Another notable feature of the new Start menu is its ability to adapt to individual user preferences. For example, users can customize the layout and organization of pinned apps by moving them, grouping them by categories, or adjusting their size to maximize space efficiency. This customization enables more efficient use of the Start menu by aligning its functionality with the specific needs and work habits of each user.

In terms of navigation, the new Windows 11 Start menu provides a smooth experience thanks to refined visual design and subtle animations that improve user interaction. Smooth transitions between menu sections and icon hover effects enhance accessibility and aesthetic appeal, making everyday use of Windows 11 more enjoyable and intuitive. These elements contribute to a consistent and modern user interface, aligned with current design standards and user expectations for usability.

Customizing the Taskbar

Customizing the taskbar in Windows 11 gives users the ability to tailor this central element of the user interface according to their individual preferences and specific needs. Unlike previous versions of Windows, the taskbar in Windows 11 is centered by default, with icons and options that can be adjusted to improve efficiency and accessibility. This customization starts with the ability to move application icons to the left or right of the taskbar, depending on user habits or ergonomic preferences.

A key aspect of taskbar customization is the ability to pin apps for quick and easy access. Users can choose the apps they use most frequently and pin them directly to the taskbar. For example, someone who regularly works with apps like Microsoft Excel, Outlook, or Spotify can pin them for instant access without having to search for the app through the Start menu or desktop.

Additionally, customizing the taskbar in Windows 11 allows users to change the size of icons to optimize space and visibility. This feature is particularly useful on displays of different resolutions or on touchscreen devices, where the size of icons can influence ease of use and ergonomics. For example, someone using a laptop with a high-resolution screen may prefer smaller icons to maximize the available workspace on the taskbar.

Users can also customize the taskbar by adding or removing things like the search box, system icons (like sound or battery), and other built-in features. This flexibility allows fine adaptation of the user interface according to the specific needs of each user. For example, some may prefer a cleaner taskbar with just a few essential icons, while others may choose to maximize the visibility of notifications and app shortcuts.

Another customization option offered by Windows 11 is the ability to automatically hide the taskbar when applications are in full-screen mode. This helps maximize the space available for the content of the application in use, while making the taskbar accessible with a simple mouse hover to the bottom of the screen. This feature is especially useful for users working on multimedia applications, games, or presentations that require distraction-free viewing.

In terms of accessibility, Windows 11 also allows users to customize the color and theme of the taskbar to match their aesthetic and functional preferences. For example, users can choose a dark theme to reduce eye strain in low-light environments, or opt for bright, contrasting colors for better visibility of icons and notifications.

Desktop and Taskbar

Organizing icons and apps

Organizing icons and apps on the desktop and taskbar in Windows 11 is critically important for maximizing productivity and ease of use. Windows 11 offers several methods for users to customize and structure their icons and applications efficiently. A common approach is pinning applications to the taskbar, which allows quick and direct access to the most used programs without having to navigate through the Start menu. For example, a user can pin apps like Microsoft Word, Excel, and Outlook for immediate access to their essential productivity tools.

In addition to the taskbar, the Windows 11 desktop offers a customizable workspace where users can organize shortcuts to their most used apps and files. This organization might include creating folders to group similar icons or strategically arranging shortcuts for intuitive navigation. For example, a user can create a folder on the desktop for graphic design applications and group shortcuts to Adobe Photoshop, Illustrator, and InDesign there for quick accessibility.

Another effective organization method is to use Windows 11 Virtual Desktops. This feature allows users to create multiple separate virtual workspaces, each with their own sets of apps and open windows. For example, a user might use one virtual desktop for project management-related tasks, another for web browsing and communication, and so on. This organization helps maintain an organized work environment and reduces confusion between open windows on a single desktop.

For more advanced management of icons on the desktop, Windows 11 allows users to customize icon size, spacing, and alignment. This feature is particularly useful for optimizing workspace on screens of different sizes and resolutions, allowing users to maximize the visibility and accessibility of important icons. For example, a user can adjust the size of icons for better readability or change the spacing between icons to avoid visual clutter.

In terms of advanced customization, Windows 11 offers options to change the icons themselves by choosing from different icon packs or customizing individual icons to match the user's aesthetic preferences. This flexibility allows for in-depth customization of the user interface, creating a unique visual experience tailored to the specific needs of each user.

Finally, finding applications quickly and efficiently is essential in a productive work environment. Windows 11 includes a built-in search feature in the Start menu and taskbar, allowing users to quickly find apps by simply entering a few characters of the name of the app they're looking for. This feature makes it easier to locate and start applications even when their icon is not directly visible on the desktop or taskbar.

Using virtual desktops

The use of virtual desktops in Windows 11 represents an advanced feature intended to improve the organization and productivity of users by allowing them to create and manage multiple distinct workspaces within the same desktop environment. Each virtual desktop can contain a unique set of open applications and windows, allowing users to visually and functionally separate different tasks or projects. For example, a user can configure one virtual desktop for software development tasks, another for project management, and a third for web browsing and communication.

Creating and managing virtual desktops in Windows 11 is simple and accessible. Users can easily add a new virtual desktop using the keyboard shortcut or clicking the dedicated icon in the taskbar. Each virtual desktop is represented by a thumbnail in the task view, allowing quick access and intuitive navigation between different desktops. This feature is particularly useful for users who juggle multiple tasks or projects simultaneously and need to maintain a clear and orderly organization of their workspace.

A significant advantage of virtual offices is their ability to reduce confusion and distraction by separating work contexts. For example, a user can focus their creative activities on a virtual desktop dedicated to graphic design or video editing, without being disturbed by notifications or irrelevant applications. This separation contributes to better concentration and increased efficiency in completing tasks.

Drag-and-drop functionality also simplifies application management between virtual desktops. Users can quickly move an open window or application from one virtual desktop to another by dragging it to the desired virtual desktop thumbnail in the task view. For example, when a user starts a new task that requires the use of different applications, they can easily move the relevant applications to a new virtual desktop without having to close or restart them.

Virtual desktops are also useful for spatial organization and workflow management. For example, a user might use one virtual desktop for everyday communication and collaboration tasks, such as email and online meetings, while reserving another virtual desktop for creative tasks and writing. This separate organization allows for a smooth transition between work contexts and better use of available office space.

In terms of customization, Windows 11 offers options for naming virtual desktops, making it easy for users to identify them based on their specific content or purpose. For example, a user can name a virtual office "Project A", another "Research and Development", and so on, for an even clearer and structured organization of their workspace.

Apps and Windows Store

Using preinstalled apps

Using pre-installed apps in Windows 11 represents an essential part of the user experience, providing a core set of software ready to use as soon as the operating system is installed. These pre-installed applications are designed to offer a range of diverse features and services, aimed at meeting common user needs without requiring additional downloads. For example, common pre-installed apps in Windows 11 include tools like the Microsoft Edge web browser, the Mail app, and various productivity apps like Microsoft Office (in some editions).

The main advantage of pre-installed applications is their immediate accessibility as soon as the operating system is installed and configured. This allows users to quickly get started with essential basic tools without having to find and install additional applications. For example, a new user can start browsing the web with Microsoft Edge the first time they use Windows 11, simplifying the process of adopting and adapting to the new computing environment.

Pre-installed apps in Windows 11 are often seamlessly integrated with other operating system features, facilitating interoperability and data synchronization. For example, the built-in calendar app lets users manage their events and appointments while automatically syncing information with other apps like Mail and Contacts. This integration reinforces the efficiency and consistency of the user experience across different daily tasks.

In addition to productivity tools, preinstalled apps often include entertainment and media apps, such as Groove Music for music library management or the Photos app for viewing and editing images. These apps provide users with a core set of features for managing and consuming media content, contributing to a complete, integrated experience on Windows 11.

Computer manufacturers and Microsoft often tailor preinstalled applications based on specific needs and regions. For example, the version of Windows 11 provided by a manufacturer may include specific local applications or customer support tools specific to their target market. This allows users to benefit from software solutions tailored to their geographic region or cultural preferences without having to seek third-party alternatives.

For some users, pre-installed apps can provide an effective and sufficient solution for their daily needs without requiring the installation of third-party apps. For example, a casual user who primarily uses the computer to browse the Internet, send emails, and manage documents may find that preinstalled apps like Edge, Mail, and Word meet their needs well without requiring further downloads or additional purchases.

Finally, although pre-installed apps offer significant benefits in terms of convenience and accessibility, some users may prefer third-party alternatives for specific functionality or personal preferences. Windows 11 allows users to personalize their experience by installing and using apps from the Microsoft Store or other third-party sources, complementing the pre-installed toolset with solutions specific to their needs.

Downloading and installing apps from the Microsoft Store

Downloading and installing apps from the Microsoft Store in Windows 11 provides a centralized and secure way for users to acquire new apps, games, and other digital content. The Microsoft Store provides a platform where developers can publish their applications, ensuring users have reliable, Microsoft-verified software. This approach aims to simplify the installation process while ensuring the security and reliability of the available applications.

To download an app from the Microsoft Store, users can browse through different categories such as recommended apps, popular games, or new releases. Each app comes with a detailed description, screenshots, and reviews from other users, providing users with essential information to make an informed decision. For example, a user looking for a photo editing app might look at the reviews and features listed before deciding to download the app.

Once an application is chosen, installation is generally done in just a few clicks. Users can check the system requirements, such as the minimum Windows version required and storage space needed, before downloading. This ensures the app is compatible with their device and avoids potential installation issues. For example, a video game application may require a specific graphics card or a minimum amount of RAM to function properly.

A key feature of the Microsoft Store is its built-in security. All applications available on the platform are subject to security checks by Microsoft, which significantly reduces the risk of installing malicious or potentially harmful software. Users can rest assured that apps downloaded from the Microsoft Store are safe and meet the strict security standards set by Microsoft. This approach builds user confidence and minimizes security risks associated with downloaded software.

Another added value of the Microsoft Store is the ability for developers to seamlessly update their apps. Users receive notifications when an update is available for an installed application, allowing them to benefit from the latest features, security fixes, and performance improvements. For example, a productivity app like Microsoft Office may receive regular updates to improve compatibility with Windows 11 and introduce new features requested by users.

In addition to apps, the Microsoft Store offers a variety of digital content such as movies, TV shows, e-books, and magazines. Users can purchase or rent this content directly from the Store, simplifying access to a diverse library of digital entertainment. This integration provides a consistent user experience where users can manage all their digital needs from a single centralized platform.

To improve the user experience, the Microsoft Store also offers personalization and recommendation options. Users can create wishlists to track apps they would like to download in the future, as well as receive personalized recommendations based on their shopping and browsing preferences. For example, a user interested in strategy games might see recommendations for similar games based on their downloads and previous interactions with the Store.

Settings and Personalization

Configuring system settings

Configuring system settings in Windows 11 is an essential step to personalize and optimize the user experience according to the specific needs of each user. System settings include a range of options that affect the overall operation of the computer, from power and device management to privacy and security. For example, users can adjust settings for sleep, screen resolution, network management, and other key features through Windows Control Panel or Settings.

An important part of configuring system settings involves power management and power saving options. Windows 11 offers various power management modes such as "Balanced", "Power Saving" and "High Performance", each of which impacts the computer's power consumption by adjusting the processor frequency and other hardware settings. For example, a user interested in extending their laptop's battery life can select "Power Saving" mode to reduce power consumption when on battery.

Screen resolution settings allow users to adjust the visual quality of their display based on the specifications of their monitor or laptop screen. Windows 11 supports a variety of screen resolutions and multi-monitor configurations, allowing users to personalize their viewing experience to maximize readability and visual comfort. For example, a user working on tasks requiring high graphics precision can adjust the screen resolution to achieve optimal detail sharpness.

Privacy and security play a crucial role in configuring system settings. Windows 11 offers detailed settings to manage app permissions, access to personal data, and online privacy. For example, users can set camera, microphone, and location data access permissions for each installed app, ensuring precise control over the privacy of their personal information.

Customization options also include configuring sound and notification settings. Users can adjust sound volume, choose specific system sounds, and manage notifications for each application to minimize interruptions and maintain concentration while using the computer. For example, a user can turn off notifications for non-essential apps during busy work periods, while keeping important alerts active.

Device management is another important component of system settings. Windows 11 allows users to configure and customize settings for connected devices such as printers, scanners, keyboards, and mice. This includes installing specific device drivers, managing advanced feature settings, and troubleshooting hardware compatibility issues. For example, a user can adjust their mouse settings to configure cursor speed and programmable buttons according to their personal preferences.

Network settings provide options for managing Internet connections and local networks. Users can configure Wi-Fi settings, manage Ethernet connections, and set file and printer sharing preferences in home or office network environments. For example, a user can prioritize certain network connections to optimize Internet connection speed and stability when streaming media content or downloading large files.

Customizing the theme and backgrounds

Customizing the theme and backgrounds in Windows 11 is an essential feature that allows users to create a visual environment tailored to their aesthetic and functional preferences. Windows 11 offers several options for customizing the overall user interface theme, including colors, backgrounds, and other visual elements. For example, users can choose from a range of predefined themes or create their own theme by adjusting main colors, accents and visual elements such as icons and sliders.

Theme customization in Windows 11 also allows you to adjust visual effects to match each user's style and preferences. This includes window transparency, blur effects, and animations when opening, closing, and minimizing windows. For example, one user may prefer unobtrusive visual effects for a smoother and faster user experience, while another may opt for more dynamic animations for a livelier aesthetic.

Color customization options give users the ability to set a consistent color palette across the entire operating system. Windows 11 provides options to adjust the accent color, window background, and other visual elements to create a harmonious and aesthetically pleasing theme. For example, a user can choose an accent color that matches their favorite brand or complements their wallpaper for a personalized viewing experience.

In addition to themes and colors, Windows 11 lets users customize their desktop background with images, slideshows, and even videos. Users can select personal images from their photo library or choose from a collection of predefined backgrounds provided by Microsoft. This flexibility allows users to transform their office into an inspiring or motivating space, tailored to their personal tastes or work environment.

Customizing backgrounds in Windows 11 also includes options to adjust the positioning and adjustment of images on the desktop. Users can choose to center, stretch, fill or tile the background image to achieve the desired visual effect. For example, a panoramic image can be stretched to fill the entire screen, while an artistic image can be positioned so that its central content is perfectly visible.

For advanced customization, Windows 11 allows users to create background slideshows by selecting multiple images to display in rotation on their desktop. Users can set how often frames change, as well as specific options like random or sequential playback order. For example, a user can create a background slideshow with vacation photos to brighten up their work day with pleasant and inspiring memories.

In terms of convenient management, Windows 11 also makes it easier to sync themes and backgrounds across multiple devices, ensuring visual consistency across desktops, laptops and tablets. Users can choose to automatically sync their personalization preferences through their Microsoft account, ensuring a smooth and consistent user experience wherever they use their devices.

Browsing and File Management

Using File Explorer

File Explorer in Windows 11 represents the primary tool for managing, browsing, and organizing files and folders on a Windows operating system. This essential tool provides users with a user-friendly and intuitive graphical interface, making it easy to access data stored locally as well as on connected devices such as external hard drives, USB drives and network drives. For example, by opening File Explorer, users can immediately view a hierarchy of folders and subfolders organized according to the structure of their file system.

A key feature of File Explorer is the ability to easily navigate through different drives, folders and subfolders using the navigation tree on the left side of the window. This allows users to quickly locate necessary files without having to remember their exact path. For example, a user can navigate from their local C: drive to an external D: drive with just a few clicks to access files stored on different media.

File Explorer also offers advanced options to sort, filter and search for specific files based on various criteria such as name, size, modification date and file type. These features make it easier to manage and organize files, especially when the volume of data is high. For example, a user can sort their files by date to quickly find the most recent documents or by type to locate all PDF files in a particular folder.

For efficient file management, File Explorer allows users to copy, move, rename and delete files and folders using simple and intuitive controls. Users can also create new folders and organize their files according to their personal or professional preferences. For example, a user can create a new folder for each project and organize the corresponding documents there for clear and structured management.

In terms of customization, Windows 11 allows users to change the appearance and behavior of File

Explorer by adjusting display options such as showing file details, icons, or thumbnails. This allows users to adapt the interface to their visual preferences and facilitate quick file recognition across different display modes. For example, a user may prefer to view thumbnails to quickly view the contents of image or video files without having to open them individually.

The integration of features like the details pane provides users with complete information about selected files, including size, type, and advanced properties such as authors and creation dates. This feature is particularly useful for meticulous file management where precise details are required. For example, a user can use the details pane to check the size of a file before copying it to an external drive with limited space.

For advanced users and system administrators, File Explorer offers advanced options such as accessing file permissions and managing previous versions, allowing granular control over security and file history. These features are essential in work environments where data security and regulatory compliance are priorities. For example, a system administrator can use these tools to manage access permissions to sensitive files and track changes to critical documents.

Managing folders and files

Managing folders and files is a fundamental skill in the daily use of operating systems like Windows 11, allowing users to efficiently organize, secure and access their digital data. Folders serve as containers for grouping related files together, making it easier to logically structure and quickly find the necessary information. For example, a user can create separate folders for individual projects, personal documents and media files to maintain a clear and efficient organization of their data.

Creating folders is a crucial first step in file management. Windows 11 lets users create folders easily from File Explorer or the desktop, allowing them to name and customize each folder according to their specific contents. For example, a user can create a folder named "Project A" to store all documents and files associated with that particular project, ensuring organized and consistent information management.

File classification involves assigning meaningful names and precise descriptions to individual files to facilitate their identification and subsequent retrieval. Windows 11 allows users to easily rename files using intuitive naming conventions, such as date, subject, or version number. For example, a user can rename a presentation file using a format such as "Presentation_ProjectA_Version1" to clearly indicate the contents and current state of the file.

Hierarchical folder organization allows users to structure their files in a way that reflects the logical relationship between different documents and information. For example, a user can create subfolders within a main folder to organize files by type (e.g. images, videos, documents) or by creation/modification date, making it easier to navigate and review. effective data management.

Copying and moving files is a common operation in data management, allowing users to transfer files between different locations for backup, sharing, or storage space management purposes. Windows 11 offers simple commands for copying and pasting files from one folder to another, as well as options for moving files while retaining associated metadata. For example, a user can copy files from a local folder to an external hard drive to backup their important data.

Secure file deletion involves not only deleting unnecessary files but also ensuring that they are permanently erased from the system to avoid unauthorized recovery or accidental data loss. Windows 11 allows users to securely delete files by using methods like the Recycle Bin or keyboard shortcuts to permanently delete files without going through the Recycle Bin. For example, a user can use the "Shift + Del" key combination to delete a file directly without moving it to the Trash.

File versioning is essential for tracking changes to a document over time, allowing users to restore previous versions if necessary. Windows 11 offers built-in features like File History that automatically saves previous versions of edited documents, making it easier to recover data when needed. For example, a user can use File History to revert to an earlier version of a document before a series of critical edits.

Finally, file security is crucial to protect sensitive information from unauthorized access or accidental loss. Windows 11 allows users to set specific access permissions for each file or folder, restricting access to authorized users only. For example, a user can configure file permissions for a confidential document by limiting access to specific team members, ensuring the confidentiality and security of sensitive information.

Multitasking and Productivity

Snap features for multitasking

The Snap features in Windows 11 represent a significant innovation for efficient multitasking on computers, giving users the ability to manage and organize multiple application windows simultaneously. This feature helps optimize the use of screen space by making it easier to position and resize windows with increased precision. For example, using Snap, a user can easily dock two windows side by side to compare documents or interact with two separate applications without having to switch between them.

One of Snap's key features is the ability to automatically resize windows when they are moved to the edge of the screen, allowing for quick and precise adjustment. For example, by dragging a window to the right side of the screen, Windows 11 automatically resizes it to occupy the right half of the screen, maximizing the space available for other tasks or applications.

The Snap Assist feature provides additional assistance by suggesting compatible open apps for snapping when the user resizes a window toward the edge of the screen. This allows for even smoother multitasking by reducing the time spent manually finding and adjusting windows. For example, when a user resizes a window to the left side of the screen, Snap Assist automatically suggests open apps to fill the remaining space, making it easier to transition between different tasks.

Virtual desktop management is enhanced with Snap, allowing users to easily create and navigate between multiple virtual desktops to organize groups of related applications or tasks. This feature is particularly useful for users who need to visually and functionally separate their workflows. For example, a user can use one virtual desktop for work tasks and another for personal activities, easily switching between them using Snap.

The Snap Layouts feature in Windows 11 provides a visual preview of the different snap layouts available when dragging a window to the edges of the screen. This allows users to quickly choose from several predefined layouts, such as quarter screen, third screen, or custom layouts, based on their specific needs. For example, a user can use Snap Layouts to divide the screen into three equal parts, with each part containing a different app for maximum productivity.

The flexibility offered by Snap allows users to customize their docking configurations based on their preferences and specific workflow. Windows 11 allows users to set custom docking rules for each app, determining how they should be positioned and resized when using Snap. For example, a user can configure a messaging app to automatically dock in the lower right corner of the screen when opened, leaving more space for other main apps.

Snap's integration with other Windows 11 features, such as virtual desktops and enhanced multitasking, makes the overall user experience more efficient. This synergy allows users to maximize their productivity by fully utilizing the multitasking capabilities of the operating system. For example, a user can arrange a virtual desktop with multiple apps anchored via Snap, then easily switch to another virtual desktop to focus on another task without confusion or distraction.

In terms of customization, Snap allows users to adjust window docking and resizing settings according to their individual preferences. Windows 11 offers options to change Snap's sensitivity and behavior, allowing for a more intuitive and personalized user experience. For example, a user can choose to disable certain Snap features or adjust the speed at which windows resize, based on their preferences and work style.

Using Windows Timeline

Windows Timeline is a feature built into Windows 11 that gives users a timeline view of their recent activities and open documents across different devices associated with their Microsoft account. This feature allows users to easily resume their previous tasks and navigate their activity history over a defined period of time. For example, a user can use Windows Timeline to quickly find a document they were recently working on, even if they have changed devices in the meantime.

Windows Timeline's timeline view spans an extended period of time, showing not only recently used applications, but also websites visited, files opened, and search activities performed. This allows users to go back in time to find information or resume tasks without having to remember their exact location. For example, a user can review their activity over the past few days to find a website visited or a file modified, thereby simplifying navigation through their digital history.

Windows Timeline synchronization across multiple Windows 11 devices enables user experience continuity, allowing users to easily move from one device to another while maintaining access to their full activity history. For example, a user can start working on a document on their desktop computer and then continue on their laptop in another location, using Windows Timeline to quickly find the document and pick up exactly where they left off.

Windows Timeline also offers advanced search capabilities, allowing users to filter their activity history by specific application, date, file type, or even keyword. This advanced search capability makes it easy to quickly locate the precise information needed, even among an extensive activity history. For example, a user can use Windows Timeline search to find all PDF documents opened in the last week, simplifying management and retrieval of important files.

Data privacy is taken into account in Windows Timeline, with the ability for users to control what activities are recorded in their history and to selectively clear items from activity history if necessary. This allows users to maintain the privacy of their personal information while still enjoying the benefits of Windows Timeline functionality. For example, a user may choose to delete specific items from their activity history for privacy or security reasons.

Windows Timeline is integrated with Windows 11's global search functionality, allowing users to quickly navigate to specific documents or apps from the timeline view or search bar. This integration facilitates smooth navigation and quick retrieval of recent items, thereby boosting user efficiency and productivity. For example, a user can search for a specific file directly from the Windows search bar and see relevant results from Windows Timeline.

For business users and those who manage multiple projects simultaneously, Windows Timeline represents a powerful tool for organizing and tracking daily activities. By making it easy to return to earlier stages of a project or review progress over time, Windows Timeline makes it easier to manage time and improve organizational efficiency. For example, a project manager can use Windows Timeline to track the progress of tasks assigned to their team and to quickly check for recent updates.

Security and Privacy

Configure basic security options

Configuring basic security options in Windows 11 is essential to protect personal data and ensure the overall security of the operating system. These options allow users to implement fundamental security measures to prevent threats such as malware, phishing attacks, and unauthorized access. One of the recommended first steps is to keep the operating system up to date by enabling automatic Windows updates. This ensures that the latest security patches and enhancements are installed regularly, reducing potential vulnerabilities exploited by cybercriminals.

Managing user accounts is another crucial security measure. Windows 11 offers several account types, including administrator accounts and standard accounts. It is recommended to limit the use of the administrator account to administrative tasks only and use a standard account for daily activities. This reduces the risk of unintentional installation of malware or unauthorized system modifications. For example, a user can create a standard account for a child to limit access to certain applications and monitor computer usage.

Setting a strong password is a standard practice to increase the security of user accounts. A strong password should include a combination of upper and lower case letters, numbers and special characters, while avoiding easily guessable personal information. Windows 11 offers built-in guidance for creating strong passwords when creating new user accounts or changing existing security settings. For example, a user can configure a strong password to access their personal account, thereby increasing resistance to brute force attacks.

Enabling and configuring Windows Firewall is another crucial measure to protect a Windows 11 PC from unauthorized network connections. Windows Firewall filters incoming and outgoing network traffic, blocking unauthorized attempts to access the computer. Users can configure firewall rules to specifically allow or block applications or network ports as needed. For example, a user can configure the firewall to block access to a suspicious application that attempts to connect to the Internet without authorization.

Malware protection is provided by Windows Defender, the built-in antivirus in Windows 11. It provides real-time protection against viruses, spyware and other threats by scanning downloaded files and applications, as well as activities running on the system. Users can schedule periodic scans or initiate manual scans to detect and remove potentially harmful malware. For example, Windows Defender can automatically block malware before it damages the system or accesses sensitive personal information.

Regular data backup is a recommended preventive measure to ensure data recovery in the event of system crashes, viruses, or accidental file loss. Windows 11 offers several options for backing up files and folders to external hard drives, network drives, or cloud storage services like OneDrive. Users can configure automatic or manual backups depending on their preferences and how often their data is updated. For example, a user can schedule a daily backup of their important files to an external drive to minimize the risk of data loss in the event of a hardware or software problem.

Safe Internet browsing is enhanced by the use of safe web browsers and awareness of safe browsing practices. Windows 11 encourages the use of modern browsers like Microsoft Edge, which includes advanced security features like tracking protection, blocking malicious sites, and password management. Users should also be aware of phishing techniques and avoid clicking on suspicious links or downloading files from unverified sources. For example, a user can enable advanced security features in Microsoft Edge to reduce the risk of exposure to malicious websites.

Finally, computer security awareness plays a crucial role in protecting against online threats. Users should be informed of basic security practices such as verifying the sources of downloads, installing software only from trusted sources, and regularly updating software and the operating system.

Windows 11 offers built-in resources and guides to educate users about common threats and security best practices. For example, a user can follow tutorials and tips offered by Windows 11 to strengthen their online security and protect their personal information.

Managing privacy settings

Managing privacy settings in Windows 11 is crucial to protect users' personal information and control how their data is collected, used and shared by the operating system and applications. Windows 11 offers a range of customizable privacy settings that allow users to determine their level of comfort and safety online. One of the recommended first steps is to review the privacy settings upon initial installation of the operating system or when updating to Windows 11, in order to customize the options according to personal preferences.

Privacy settings in Windows 11 cover various aspects, including credentials management, device access, location, voice and inking, diagnostics, and usage data. For example, users can choose to limit app access to location data or restrict Microsoft's collection of diagnostic data to improve the overall privacy of their system. This granularity allows users to specifically control what information is shared with the operating system and third-party applications.

Managing privacy settings also includes the ability to manage individual app permissions. Windows 11 allows users to view and change the permissions granted to each installed app, such as access to files, cameras, microphones, and other devices. For example, a user can revoke an app's access to their camera if they don't feel comfortable with the app using that feature.

Personal data protection is enhanced by advanced privacy options such as cookie and tracker management in the Microsoft Edge browser. Users can enable strict privacy settings to limit online tracking by websites and targeted ads. For example, by enabling Strict mode in Microsoft Edge, a user can automatically block third-party trackers and thus improve the privacy of their internet browsing.

Account data privacy is a major concern for many users. Windows 11 offers enhanced security options such as multi-factor authentication to protect access to Microsoft accounts. This feature adds an extra layer of security by requiring additional verification, such as a code sent via SMS or biometric verification, when signing in to a Microsoft account from a new device or app. For example, a user can configure multi-factor authentication for their Microsoft account to further secure access to their personal and financial information.

Managing privacy settings also extends to children and family, with specific options for controlling access and monitoring children's online activities. Windows 11 offers built-in parental controls tools that allow parents to limit access to certain content, track online activity, and manage children's screen time. For example, a parent can set screen time limits and block access to inappropriate apps or websites to ensure their children's safety and digital well-being.

Transparency and education are important aspects of managing privacy settings in Windows 11. Microsoft provides detailed information about what data is collected, why it is collected, and how it is used for personalization or advertising. improvement of services. Users can access privacy reports to understand how their data is managed and make informed decisions about which privacy settings to apply. For example, a user might visit the Microsoft Trust Center for information about the company's privacy practices and data management policies.

Finally, compliance with data protection regulations such as the General Data Protection Regulation (GDPR) is a priority for Windows 11. Microsoft is committed to upholding the highest privacy standards and providing users with tools to exercise their data protection rights, such as access to collected personal data or the right to erasure of data. For example, a European user may exercise their right of access to obtain a copy of their personal data held by Microsoft in accordance with GDPR requirements.

Connection and Networks

Configuring and managing network connections

Configuring and managing network connections in Windows 11 is critically important to ensure reliable and secure connectivity for both home users and business environments. Windows 11 offers a user-friendly interface and advanced tools that allow users to configure, monitor and troubleshoot network issues efficiently. One of the first steps in setting up a network connection is to identify the type of network the computer is connected to: home network, public network, or work network. Each type of network may require different security and file sharing settings. For example, a user may configure a home network to share files between different devices while a public network may restrict these features for security reasons.

Managing network connections in Windows 11 includes configuring IP and DNS settings. Users can choose between automatically assigning an IP

63

address by the Dynamic Host Configuration Protocol (DHCP) server or manually configuring IP addresses, depending on specific network needs. Likewise, configuring DNS servers allows domain names to be resolved into IP addresses, essential for accessing websites and online services. For example, a user can change TCP/IP settings to set a static IP address on their networked computer for easier identification and communication with other devices.

Network connection security is enhanced by the use of Wi-Fi Protected Access 3 (WPA3) for wireless networks, providing advanced protection against brute force attacks and malicious interception. Windows 11 supports WPA3 for secure Wi-Fi connections, ensuring the confidentiality of data exchanged between the computer and the wireless access point. Users can configure strong passwords and advanced security options to secure their home or business Wi-Fi network. For example, a network administrator can deploy WPA3 security settings on a corporate network to protect sensitive employee communications.

Advanced network management includes the ability to create virtual local area networks (VLANs) to isolate different groups of users or devices within the same physical network. VLANs allow you to segment network traffic and apply specific security policies to each group, improving performance management and overall network security. For example, a system administrator can configure VLANs to separate finance and marketing departments within a company to limit access to sensitive data to authorized users only.

Monitoring network performance is made easy by using built-in tools such as Windows 11 Task Manager, which displays real-time network statistics, including download and upload speed, network usage per application, and information about connected network adapters. This visibility allows users to diagnose network performance issues, such as slow speeds or congestion, and take appropriate corrective action. For example, a user can use Task Manager to identify an application consuming a large amount of bandwidth and adjust its network usage settings.

Troubleshooting network issues is made simple with Windows 11's Network Troubleshooter, an automatic tool that identifies and fixes common network connectivity issues. Network Troubleshooting Assistant analyzes network configurations, adapters, and IP settings to detect potential errors and suggests solutions to resolve them. For example, Network Troubleshooting Assistant can reset the network adapter or renew the IP address to restore connectivity after a service interruption.

Virtual Private Network (VPN) connection management is a feature built into Windows 11, allowing users to secure their online communications and securely access a company's network resources remotely. Users can configure VPN connections to establish a secure tunnel between their computer and a remote server, protecting data from interception by unauthorized third parties. For example, a traveling professional can use a VPN connection to securely access company files and applications from a public Wi-Fi network.

Finally, centralized group policy management (GPO) in business environments allows network administrators to define and enforce consistent security rules across all computers and users in the Windows domain. GPOs allow you to automatically configure network settings, apply access restrictions, and secure network connections in accordance with company security policies. For example, a network administrator can use GPOs to disable certain network features on all computers in a domain to strengthen overall network security.

Using Bluetooth and other devices

Using Bluetooth and other peripherals in Windows 11 provides increased flexibility to connect and use a variety of devices wirelessly, making it easier for users to interact with their devices. Bluetooth, in particular, is widely used to connect peripherals such as mice, keyboards, headphones, printers, and smartphones to a Windows 11 computer. The Bluetooth pairing process involves putting the devices into discovery mode and select the appropriate device from the list of detected devices. For example, a user can pair Bluetooth headphones to their computer to listen to music wirelessly or participate in video calls.

Advanced Bluetooth features in Windows 11 include support for specific profiles such as Hands-Free Profile (HFP) for voice calls and Advanced Audio Distribution Profile (A2DP) for high-quality audio streaming. These profiles allow users to enjoy a rich and clear audio experience while using Bluetooth-enabled devices. For example, a user can use a Bluetooth speaker supported by the A2DP profile to stream music with higher sound quality from their computer.

Device management in Windows 11 extends beyond Bluetooth to include other wireless technologies such as USB Wi-Fi dongles, IR (infrared) adapters, and video capture devices. These devices can be connected and configured through the Windows 11 Device Manager, providing seamless integration and ease of use for users. For example, a user can install a USB Wi-Fi dongle to extend their computer's wireless connectivity, allowing them to access the Internet from any available Wi-Fi hotspot.

External device connectivity is simplified by using Windows 11's Plug and Play feature, which automatically detects newly connected devices and installs the necessary drivers to ensure proper compatibility and operation. This plug-and-play capability allows users to plug in peripherals such as USB drives, external hard drives, and card readers without needing to restart the computer or perform additional configurations. For example, a user can plug a USB mouse into their computer and start using it immediately without any manual intervention.

Managing device settings in Windows 11 allows users to optimize the performance and functionality of their connected devices. Through Control Panel or Modern Settings in Windows 11, users can adjust mouse sensitivity settings, Bluetooth connection speed, screen resolution configurations for external monitors, and many other options specific to each type of device. For example, a user can customize the keyboard shortcuts of their gaming mouse for precise adjustments during intensive gaming sessions.

Device security is a key concern in Windows 11, where users are encouraged to check device security certificates before connecting them to their computer. Security certificates ensure that devices are authentic and have not been tampered with or compromised by malware. Additionally, regular device driver updates are essential to ensure the continued compatibility and security of devices connected to Windows 11. For example, a user can check for available driver updates for their printer to benefit from the latest updates. latest features and security fixes.

Advanced device management in business environments is made easier through the use of Group Policies (GPO) in Windows 11, allowing network administrators to set security rules and access restrictions for devices connected to business computers. business. GPOs help limit the use of unauthorized devices or restrict access to USB ports to prevent sensitive data leaks. For example, a network administrator can configure

GPOs to prevent the use of unsecured USB devices in corporate offices to increase the security of confidential information.

Finally, device interoperability with Windows 11 is improved with universal connectivity standards such as USB-C and Thunderbolt, which provide fast data transfer speeds and broad compatibility with a diverse range of devices. Users can connect external displays, docking stations, hard drives, and other accessories through these standard interfaces, simplifying the experience of using devices with Windows 11. For example, a user can use a Thunderbolt adapter to connect a 4K monitor to your Windows 11 laptop and benefit from an immersive, high-resolution visual experience.

Backup and Recovery

Autosave options

Automatic backup options in Windows 11 provide users with a reliable method to preserve their important data in the event of a system failure, accidental file deletion, or any other unforeseen incident. This essential feature allows users to set up regular, automated backups of their files, ensuring continued protection against critical data loss. Automatic backup options can be configured to back up different types of data, including documents, photos, videos and system settings, providing peace of mind and guaranteed recovery when needed.

Windows 11 offers several methods for setting up automatic backups, including using the built-in Backup and Restore tool as well as cloud storage solutions like OneDrive. The "Backup and Restore" tool allows users to schedule regular backups to external drives or network drives. For example, a user can set up a daily backup of their important documents to an external hard drive to protect against data loss due to hardware failures.

Automatic backups can be customized to include specific settings such as frequency of backups, file types to back up, and folders to include or exclude. This flexibility allows users to tailor their backups according to their individual needs and the nature of their critical data. For example, a user might choose to back up only their work documents and leave out large media files to save storage space.

Managing automatic backups in Windows 11 also includes the ability to quickly restore backed up data when needed. The "Backup and Restore" tool allows users to restore individual files or entire datasets from previously created backups. For example, if an important file is accidentally deleted, the user can easily recover it from the most recent backup.

Users can also benefit from integration with OneDrive to automatically back up their files to the cloud. OneDrive offers a secure backup solution accessible from any Internet-connected device, ensuring constant data availability. For example, a user can enable OneDrive's auto-backup feature to sync their documents and photos across all their Windows 11 devices and easily access them from anywhere.

Data security is a priority in Windows 11's automatic backup options. Users can enable backup encryption to protect their sensitive data from unauthorized access. This feature ensures increased confidentiality of personal and professional information stored in backups. For example, a user can use BitLocker encryption to secure an external hard drive used for automatic backups, ensuring sensitive data is protected.

Scheduling automatic backups in Windows 11 is a recommended practice to ensure efficient management of system resources and continued data protection. Users can set backup schedules that minimize the impact on computer performance during periods of heavy use. For example, a user can schedule a daily automatic backup overnight to avoid any interruptions during work hours.

Backup notifications and reports provide users with detailed information on the status of automatic backups, including files backed up, any errors, and backup successes. These notifications allow users to stay informed about the health of their backups and to intervene quickly in the event of a problem. For example, a user can receive a notification if an automatic backup fails due to a connectivity issue with the backup device.

Finally, centralized management of automatic backups in business environments is simplified through the use of Group Policies (GPO) in Windows 11. Network administrators can configure and enforce consistent backup policies across the corporate network, ensuring thus compliance with security requirements and uniform protection of sensitive data. For example, a network administrator can deploy GPOs to ensure that all Windows 11 devices in the company perform regular automatic backups to dedicated servers to minimize the risk of data loss.

Using Windows 11 Recovery Tools

Using Windows 11 recovery tools is crucial to restore the operating system to a functional state after incidents such as hardware failures, critical system errors, or malware infections. These integrated tools provide users with a variety of ways to diagnose, repair and restore their system without the need for a complete reinstallation, thereby minimizing downtime and preserving important personal data.

One of the essential tools is Windows 11's "PC Reset" feature, which allows you to reinstall the operating system while keeping or deleting personal files as per the user's choice. This option is useful for troubleshooting persistent performance issues or serious system errors. For example, a user may choose to reset their PC while retaining their personal documents to restore the system to a stable state.

"Safe Mode" is another powerful tool that allows you to start Windows 11 with a minimal set of drivers and services, ideal for diagnosing and fixing software or hardware compatibility issues. This mode restricts running programs, making it easier to identify potential causes of problems. For example, a user can boot into Safe Mode to uninstall a recently installed driver that is causing instabilities in the system.

For situations where Windows 11 fails to boot properly, the "Startup Repair" tool can be used to fix startup errors and restore the system's bootability. This tool automatically scans and repairs problems related to damaged or missing startup files, allowing the computer to restart normally. For example, after an unsuccessful Windows update, the user can use the Startup Repair tool to restore startup functionality without having to reinstall the operating system.

"System Restore" is a feature that allows users to revert to a previously created restore point, which undoes recent system changes without affecting the user's personal files. This option is particularly useful for correcting problems caused by incorrectly applied software changes or driver updates. For example, if a software update causes critical errors, the user can restore the system to a previous functional state.

The "System Image Recovery" tool allows users to completely restore the system from a previously created system image. A system image is a complete copy of the hard drive or system partition at a given point in time, capturing the state of the operating system, installed applications, and personal files. For example, after a severe hardware crash, the user can restore their system from a previously saved system image to return to their work or gaming environment without losing data.

Windows 11 also offers advanced command line tools like "SFC" (System File Checker) and "DISM" (Deployment Image Servicing and Management) to repair corrupted or missing system files. SFC checks the integrity of critical system files and automatically replaces them with correct versions from a protected cache, while DISM is used to repair Windows deployment image from installation sources. For example, a user can run SFC to resolve system errors that cause frequent system crashes.

Creating external recovery media is a recommended practice for accessing Windows 11 recovery tools when the primary system is inaccessible. Users can create USB recovery drive or DVD/CD system recovery disc from Windows recovery settings. This external media allows you to boot the computer from it and access recovery options even if the operating system is damaged. For example, a user can use a USB recovery drive to access the Startup Repair tool and restore Windows 11 startup functionality.

Finally, advanced users and system administrators can benefit from the Deployment Image Management and Servicing (DISM) tool to capture, modify, and deploy Windows operating system images. DISM allows you to create custom Windows images with specific configurations, built-in updates, and pre-installed applications for uniform distribution across multiple machines. For example, a system administrator can use DISM to prepare a customized Windows 11 image with specific security settings and applications before deploying it to multiple desktops in an enterprise network.

Maintenance and Updates

Managing system updates

Managing system updates in Windows 11 is critically important to ensure the security, performance, and reliability of the operating system. Systematic updates include security fixes, functional enhancements and performance optimizations that are essential to maintaining a robust and secure IT environment. Microsoft regularly releases updates through Windows Update to address newly discovered security vulnerabilities and improve existing features, ensuring continued threat protection and an improved user experience.

Security updates are among the most critical types of system updates. They are designed to fix potential security vulnerabilities that could be exploited by malware to compromise system security. For example, Microsoft's monthly security patches for Windows 11 aim to address critical vulnerabilities discovered by security researchers and Microsoft teams, ensuring that users are protected against current threats.

In addition to security updates, Windows 11 also offers functional updates that introduce new features, user interface improvements, and performance optimizations. These updates may include improvements to device management, system performance, and built-in applications like the Microsoft Edge browser. For example, a recent functional update introduced significant improvements to virtual desktop management and user interface customization options.

Update scheduling in Windows 11 is optimized to minimize work interruptions and maximize usability. Users can configure maintenance hours during which the system automatically installs updates without disrupting ongoing operations. This flexibility allows users to schedule updates during periods of low usage, such as non-working hours or at night. For example, a user can set a weekly maintenance window so that updates are installed automatically overnight.

Windows 11 users can choose between automatic and manual update options based on their preferences and security requirements. The automatic update option is recommended to ensure systems are constantly protected against emerging threats, while the manual option allows users to specifically control when and how updates are installed. For example, in a business environment, system administrators can configure group policies to manage automatic updates on employee workstations according to company policies.

Managing system updates in Windows 11 also includes the ability to roll back previously installed updates in case of compatibility issues or malfunctions after installing a new update. This feature allows users to return to a stable system state and defer the installation of problematic updates until a suitable solution is available. For example, a user can uninstall an update that caused compatibility issues with critical software until a fix is released.

Driver updates are a crucial aspect of managing system updates in Windows 11, as they ensure the compatibility and performance of connected hardware devices. Microsoft works with device manufacturers to certify and distribute the latest drivers through Windows Update, ensuring smooth device integration with the operating system. For example, a recent driver update could improve the stability and performance of a graphics card, thereby optimizing a computer's graphics capabilities.

Centralized management of system updates is made easier by using Microsoft management services such as Microsoft Endpoint Configuration Manager (MECM), formerly SCCM. MECM allows IT administrators to deploy, manage and monitor updates across complex enterprise networks, ensuring that all Windows 11 devices are kept up to date securely and consistently. For example, a network administrator can use MECM to plan and deploy critical updates across the entire enterprise IT fleet according to a pre-established schedule and specific deployment rules.

Optimizing your PC performance

Optimizing the performance of a Windows 11 PC is essential to ensure a smooth and responsive user experience, maximizing the efficiency of available hardware and software resources. This optimization involves a combination of practices and tools aimed at improving processing speed, system responsiveness, and resource management.

First, performance analysis using Windows 11's built-in "Resource Monitor" tool allows users to view which apps and processes are consuming the most resources such as CPU, memory, and disk . This analysis provides valuable information to identify bottlenecks and optimize the use of available resources. For example, by identifying a resource-consuming application, a user can decide to close or uninstall it to improve overall system performance.

Second, managing programs at startup is crucial to reduce system startup time and free up resources at startup. Windows 11 lets users manage auto-starting apps through the Task Manager, disabling non-essential programs on startup. For example, by disabling auto-updating applications or unused utilities, users can reduce the initial load on the system and improve overall response time.

Third, hard disk defragmentation can significantly improve data reading and writing performance by reorganizing fragmented files on the disk. Although modern SSDs require defragmentation less often due to their different storage structure, traditional hard drives can benefit from this periodic optimization. For example, by scheduling regular defragmentation using Windows 11's "Disk Defragmenter" tool, users can maintain optimal disk performance and reduce application load times.

Fourth, virtual memory management is an important practice to optimize system performance, especially when physical memory (RAM) is limited. Windows 11 uses virtual memory to allocate disk space as an extension of RAM when needed. Users can manually adjust the virtual memory size to match their system's specific needs, improving resource management and overall responsiveness. For example, by increasing the size of virtual memory on a fast disk, users can compensate for the lack of physical RAM and maintain smooth performance when running memory-intensive applications.

Fifth, managing power settings can significantly influence PC performance by adjusting power consumption and CPU performance. Windows 11 offers several preconfigured power plans such as "Balanced" and "High Performance", as well as the ability to customize these settings. For example, users can choose the "High Performance" plan when they need to maximize performance for demanding tasks like gaming or video editing, or opt for the "Power Saving" plan to extend the battery life on laptops.

Sixth, updating device drivers is crucial to ensure optimal hardware compatibility and performance in Windows 11. Updated drivers can fix bugs, improve stability, and offer new features. Windows Update often automates updating common drivers, but users can also manually download and install the latest versions from the device manufacturer's site. For example, installing an updated graphics driver can improve graphics rendering performance in 3D applications and games.

Seventh, the management of animations and visual effects can have a significant impact on the responsiveness and smoothness of the system. Windows 11 offers options to adjust or disable visual effects such as animation transitions, shadows, and transparency effects. By reducing these visual effects, users can reduce the load on the CPU and graphics card, improving application and system response times. For example, by disabling window animations, a user may notice a noticeable increase in navigation speed between windows and applications.

Finally, optimizing search and indexing settings can improve the speed and accuracy of search results in Windows 11. Windows Search indexes files and folders to speed up searches, but this can affect performance, especially on slower hard drives. Users can adjust indexing settings to exclude certain non-essential folders or file types, thereby optimizing the use of system resources. For example, by limiting indexing to frequently used folders, users can reduce disk load and speed up response times when searching for files.

Accessibility and Special Features

Built-in accessibility options

The built-in accessibility options in Windows 11 play a crucial role in allowing users to customize the interface and features of the operating system to meet various accessibility needs. These features are designed to improve visual, auditory, motor and cognitive accessibility, ensuring inclusive and effective use of the system for all users, regardless of their ability level.

First, Windows 11 offers visual accessibility options such as screen magnification, which allows users to zoom in on part of the screen to make it easier to read text and see details. This zoom can be activated using keyboard shortcuts or touch gestures, providing flexibility of use. For example, a visually impaired user can enlarge the screen to see the content of an application or website more clearly without losing important details.

Second, the high contrast options in Windows 11 change the colors and contrast of the user interface to improve the readability of text and visual elements. Users can choose from different high-contrast themes or customize colors according to their visual preferences. This feature is especially useful for people with color blindness or visual impairments who require increased contrast to distinguish elements on the screen.

Third, built-in narration in Windows 11 allows the system to read content displayed on the screen aloud, making information easier to access for users who are visually impaired or have reading difficulties. This feature can be enabled to read text in apps, web pages and documents, providing valuable assistance in understanding written content. For example, a user with reading difficulties can use narration to listen to the content of an email or online article.

Fourth, Windows 11 includes hearing accessibility options such as real-time transcription of dialogue in videos using automatic captioning technology. This feature allows deaf or hard of hearing users to follow conversations in videos in real time, improving accessibility to multimedia content. For example, when broadcasting a video presentation, automatic subtitles can be activated to display the text of the dialogues, ensuring complete understanding of the content for all viewers.

Fifth, keyboard and mouse options in Windows 11 allow advanced customization to meet the needs of users with motor difficulties or mobility disorders. These options include key repeats, cursor speed, and simplified mouse gestures to make it easier to navigate and interact with the interface. For example, users can adjust the keyboard key repeat speed to accommodate users with dexterity difficulties.

Sixth, Windows 11 offers cognitive accessibility features such as Easy Reading, which helps reduce the complexity of text displayed on the screen by removing unnecessary elements and highlighting essential information. This feature is beneficial for users with information processing or comprehension disorders, making reading and concentration easier. For example, easy reading can be enabled to make instructions and technical documents more accessible.

Seventh, customizable keyboard shortcuts and touch gestures in Windows 11 provide increased flexibility for interacting with the system, allowing users to set specific commands tailored to their accessibility needs. These shortcuts can be used to quickly navigate between apps, enable accessibility features, or perform common tasks without relying on the traditional interface. For example, a user can configure a keyboard shortcut to quickly activate magnifier or narration based on their specific needs.

Finally, Windows 11 supports third-party tools and apps to further expand the accessibility options available. Microsoft Store offers a variety of accessible apps designed to meet specific needs such as augmented communication, voice control, and vision-free navigation. These add-on apps allow users to personalize their accessibility experience based on their unique needs. For example, a user can download a symbol communication application to facilitate social and professional interaction.

Use of tools for specific needs

Using tools to address specific needs is crucial to enabling diverse users to get the most out of their Windows 11 computing experience. These tools are designed to address a diverse range of needs, ranging from accessibility and ergonomics to productivity and customization, thus ensuring efficient and personalized use of the operating system.

First, the accessibility tools built into Windows 11 play a vital role in allowing users with different abilities to interact with their computers comfortably and efficiently. For example, the narration tool can be used by visually impaired users to hear the content displayed on the screen, improving accessibility to digital information.

Second, UI customization tools allow users to change the way Windows 11 looks and works based on their individual preferences. These tools include customizing themes, wallpapers, icons, and accent colors. For example, a user can adjust high contrast settings to make the screen more readable or choose a dark theme to reduce eye strain during prolonged use.

Third, productivity management tools like Microsoft Office and OneDrive make it easy to create, edit and share documents, spreadsheets and presentations. These tools are integrated into the Windows 11 ecosystem, providing seamless data synchronization and real-time collaboration between users. For example, a professional can use Microsoft Teams to hold virtual meetings and share documents with remote colleagues.

Fourth, security and data management tools play a crucial role in ensuring the protection of sensitive information and compliance with privacy regulations. Windows 11 offers features like Windows Defender, built-in antivirus, and disk encryption options to secure critical data. For example, a user can configure BitLocker to encrypt hard drives and protect personal data from unauthorized access.

Fifth, development and programming tools in Windows 11 are essential for developers and IT professionals. Integrated development environment (IDE) like Visual Studio provides advanced features for creating software applications, debugging, and deploying to various platforms. For example, a developer can use Visual Studio to design and test Windows 11 apps optimized for new operating system features.

Sixth, network and Internet connection management tools are important for optimizing the performance and security of network connections in Windows 11. These tools include Network Manager and Network Troubleshooter, which allow users to diagnose and troubleshoot connectivity issues. For example, a network administrator can use these tools to configure advanced network settings and ensure secure access to shared resources.

Seventh, file and memory management tools are essential to effectively organize and manage data on a Windows 11 PC. File Explorer offers an intuitive interface for navigating directories, copying, moving and deleting files , as well as to manage storage settings. For example, a user can use Disk Cleanup tools to free up storage space or archive files into organized folders.

Finally, data backup and recovery tools are critical to preventing data loss and ensuring business continuity. Windows 11 offers solutions like File History and Windows Backup and Restore to automatically back up important files and restore systems after a failure. For example, a user can configure File History to regularly back up their personal documents to an external drive, ensuring protection against unexpected data loss.

Tips and Tricks for Windows 11

Tips for more efficient use

To maximize the efficiency of using Windows 11, it is crucial to adopt practices and tips that help maximize productivity while minimizing potential frustrations with the operating system's interface and performance. These tips cover various aspects of user experience, from desktop organization to optimizing PC performance.

First, organizing the office efficiently can greatly improve productivity. Using Windows 11 virtual desktops to group related apps and tasks can help maintain an orderly work environment. For example, dedicating a virtual desktop to work applications, another to leisure activities, and so on, makes it easy to move from one context to another without cluttering the main workspace.

Second, taking advantage of keyboard shortcuts can significantly speed up common tasks. Windows

11 offers a range of keyboard shortcuts for quickly navigating between windows, opening specific apps, and performing actions like taking a screenshot or managing windows. For example, using the Windows + Tab key combination to switch between virtual desktops or Ctrl + Shift + Esc to open the Task Manager can save valuable time in daily operations.

Third, customizing the Start menu and taskbar can make access to frequently used applications and tools more efficient. Pinning important apps to the taskbar allows quick access without having to search through the Start menu. Additionally, organizing apps into groups or folders on the Start menu makes navigation and searching easier. For example, grouping applications by categories such as "Office", "Multimedia", and "Development Tools" can simplify search and selection.

Fourth, intelligently managing system notifications and alerts can reduce distractions and maintain focus. Using Windows 11 notification settings to filter alerts based on priority and turning off notifications for less critical apps during busy work periods can improve productivity. For example, prioritizing notifications from work messaging apps while reducing notifications from social media during work hours helps you stay focused on important tasks.

Fifth, keeping the system updated by regularly installing Windows 11 updates is crucial to benefit from the latest security features, bug fixes and performance improvements. Enabling automatic updates ensures that the PC remains protected against vulnerabilities and performs optimally. For example, security updates can fix critical vulnerabilities that could be exploited by malware, keeping personal and business data safe.

Sixth, using Windows 11's advanced search features can help quickly locate files, apps, and even system settings. The integrated search bar in the Start menu allows searching both locally on the PC and online, providing a convenient solution for quickly accessing the necessary information. For example, by simply typing the name of a file into the search bar, the user can find and open the document without having to navigate through folders.

Seventh, securing the PC with additional protection measures like enabling disk encryption with BitLocker can enhance the security of sensitive data. BitLocker allows you to encrypt internal and external hard drives, ensuring that even if the device is lost or stolen, the data remains inaccessible to unauthorized third parties. For example, a professional can encrypt their external drive containing confidential information before transporting it out of the office.

Finally, regularly backing up important data is essential to prevent data loss in the event of a hardware failure or unforeseen incident. Using backup solutions like File History or cloud services like OneDrive can quickly restore files when needed. For example, scheduling regular automatic backups of critical documents ensures that the most recent versions are always available in case something goes wrong.

Useful keyboard shortcuts

Keyboard shortcuts are essential tools for improving user efficiency and productivity in Windows 11. By using specific key combinations, users can quickly perform common actions, navigate between apps, and access various features without having to to use the mouse. This approach not only saves time, but also allows smoother interaction with the operating system.

First, keyboard shortcuts allow you to quickly navigate between open applications. For example, using Alt + Tab, users can quickly switch between active windows without going to the taskbar. This feature is particularly useful when there are several applications open simultaneously and it is necessary to quickly switch from one task to another.

Second, window management shortcuts simplify workspace organization. For example, Windows + Left or Right Arrow moves the active window to the left or right of the screen, making it easier to set up a multi-window layout for better task management.

Third, shortcuts for managing files and folders provide quick ways to copy, cut, paste and delete items. For example, Ctrl + C for copy, Ctrl + X for cut, and Ctrl + V for paste are universally used key combinations that speed up file management operations.

Fourth, shortcuts for screenshot functions allow users to easily capture part of the screen or the entire screen without having to open any additional applications. For example, Windows + Shift + S opens the Quick Screenshot tool, providing options to select a specific area or capture the entire screen.

Fifth, keyboard shortcuts for accessing system settings allow users to quickly customize their Windows experience. For example, Windows + I directly opens Windows Settings where users can adjust personalization, security, and update options without having to navigate through multiple menus.

Sixth, keyboard shortcuts for media management allow you to control audio and video playback directly from the keyboard. For example, the F9,

F10, and F11 keys can be used to control play, pause, and full screen in media players and web browsers.

Seventh, keyboard shortcuts for specific applications provide quick access to advanced features. For example, in Microsoft Word, Ctrl + S saves the active document, while Ctrl + P opens the print dialog box, providing direct access to frequently used actions.

Finally, keyboard shortcuts for web browsing improve the user experience when browsing the Internet. For example, Ctrl + T opens a new tab in the web browser, while Ctrl + Tab switches between open tabs, providing quick and efficient navigation.

Troubleshooting and Common Problems

Solutions to startup problems

When boot problems occur on a Windows 11 system, it is crucial to understand the potential causes and the appropriate resolution steps to restore the PC to normal operation. Boot problems can be caused by a variety of factors, from software errors to hardware issues, and often require a methodical approach to effectively diagnose and resolve the problem.

First of all, boot errors can sometimes be caused by incorrectly installed software updates or corrupted drivers. When the Windows 11 system fails to boot properly after an update, it is recommended to use the built-in recovery options to restore the system to an earlier point before the update was installed. For example, accessing Advanced Boot Options by pressing F8 or Shift + F8 during startup can select the System Restore option.

Second, boot problems may be related to misconfigured BIOS or UEFI settings. Checking and updating boot settings in the BIOS can resolve hardware conflicts or configuration errors that are preventing the system from loading properly. For example, resetting BIOS settings to default or checking secure boot configurations can fix configuration errors.

Third, boot errors can be caused by bad sectors on the hard drive or damaged partitions. Using the built-in Disk Diagnostic Tool or third-party tools to check disk integrity and repair bad sectors can resolve issues related to read and write errors. For example, running CHKDSK with repair option can recover and repair disk errors.

Fourth, malware infections can also cause boot problems by corrupting critical system files or changing startup settings. Using antivirus software to perform a full system scan and eliminate any detected threats is essential. For example, booting into safe mode and running an antivirus scan can identify and remove malware before it causes further damage to the system.

Fifth, hardware issues such as motherboard, RAM, or hard drive failures can cause improper boot symptoms. Performing a thorough hardware diagnosis using appropriate diagnostic tools or testing each component individually can help identify and replace faulty parts. For example, using tools like MemTest86 to test RAM or CrystalDiskInfo to check hard drive health can provide valuable information about the health of the hardware.

Sixth, startup errors can also be caused by conflicts between third-party applications or services started automatically with Windows. Disabling non-essential autostart programs or booting into safe mode to isolate the problem can help identify the application responsible for the errors. For example, using Task Manager to disable startup programs or booting into Safe Mode with Networking to diagnose software compatibility issues.

Seventh, boot errors related to Windows updates can sometimes be resolved by performing a system reset or restore. Using advanced recovery options to restore the system to a previous state before the faulty update was installed can often restore the system to normal operation. For example, accessing advanced recovery options through Windows Settings can restore the system to a previous restore point.

Finally, if all troubleshooting methods fail, completely reinstalling the operating system using Windows 11 installation media may be necessary. This approach can help bypass serious system errors or irreparable damage caused by malware infections or hard drive errors. For example, creating Windows 11 USB installation media and reinstalling the system following the installation steps can restore a clean and working system.

Troubleshooting common system errors

Troubleshooting common system errors in Windows 11 requires a thorough understanding of potential causes and proper methods to diagnose and resolve issues. System errors can affect various aspects of operating system operation, ranging from boot problems to application and device malfunctions. A methodical and knowledgeable approach is essential to minimize the impact of these errors and restore system stability.

First, errors related to Windows updates are among the most common. When updates fail or cause conflicts with drivers or applications, it can cause operational errors. Using the built-in recovery options to restore the system to a previous restore point before the problematic updates were installed is often effective. For example, accessing Windows 11's advanced recovery settings allows you to uninstall recent updates and restore system stability.

Secondly, registry errors can occur when incorrect or corrupt entries affect the system configuration. Using reliable registry cleaning tools can help identify and fix these errors. For example, programs like CCleaner offer features to clean the Windows registry and fix potential errors that could compromise system performance.

Third, errors related to device drivers can lead to malfunctions, crashes, or blue screens (BSOD). Updating device drivers through Device Manager or the manufacturer's website can resolve these issues. For example, installing the latest NVIDIA or AMD graphics drivers can improve compatibility with Windows 11 and prevent display-related errors.

Fourth, errors related to corrupted or missing system files can prevent the system from functioning properly. Using the System File Checker (SFC) tool or the Deployment Image Servicing and Management (DISM) command can repair these files. For example, running the SFC /scannow command in Command Prompt as administrator can identify and repair damaged system files.

Fifth, hard drive errors, such as bad sectors or damaged partitions, can cause system instabilities. Using disk diagnostic tools like CHKDSK can help check and repair hard drive errors. For example, running CHKDSK with the repair option can fix read/write errors and restore file system integrity.

Sixth, boot errors can result from incorrect BIOS settings or incompatible hardware configurations. Checking and updating BIOS settings to ensure hardware compatibility and stability is essential. For example, resetting BIOS settings to default or adjusting Secure Boot configurations can prevent boot errors and improve overall system performance.

Seventh, network errors like Wi-Fi or Ethernet connection issues can be fixed by resetting network adapters or updating network drivers. Using Windows 11's built-in Network Troubleshooter can also diagnose and fix connectivity issues. For example, resetting the network settings to their original state or disabling/re-enabling the network adapter can restore the internet connection.

Finally, errors related to third-party applications can also disrupt the normal functioning of the system. Uninstalling recently installed or problematic applications, or booting into safe mode to isolate the problem, can help identify the source of errors. For example, using Task Manager to disable nonessential autostart programs can prevent software conflicts and improve system stability.

Migrating from Windows 10

Windows 11 upgrade process

The Windows 11 upgrade process represents a significant transition for users looking to benefit from the new features and improvements brought by this operating system. This upgrade involves several essential steps to ensure a smooth and successful transition, while minimizing potential disruption to users' computing environments. Understanding these steps and the prerequisites is crucial to optimizing the user experience throughout the process.

First of all, it is essential to check if the current system meets the minimum requirements of Windows 11. These requirements include hardware specifications such as compatibility with TPM 2.0 (Trusted Platform Module), as well as processor criteria, RAM and storage space. For example, a processor compatible with 8th generation Intel

Core or AMD Ryzen is required to take advantage of advanced features in Windows 11.

Next, a hardware and device compatibility assessment should be performed to ensure that all system components will be fully supported after the upgrade. Some devices may require updated drivers or specific configurations to work properly in Windows 11. For example, graphics card drivers and audio drivers must be compatible with new Windows 11 features and architecture to ensure optimal performance. optimal.

Once hardware compatibility is confirmed, users can consider upgrading using available tools, such as Windows Update Assistant or the Installation Media Creation Tool. These tools allow you to download and install Windows 11 while preserving existing data and applications wherever possible. For example, Windows Update Assistant guides users through the upgrade process by checking compatibility and downloading the necessary files.

Before proceeding with the installation, it is recommended to back up all important data and create a system image or full system backup. Although upgrading to Windows 11 is designed to preserve personal files, it is prudent to take extra precautions to avoid unexpected data loss. For example, using third-party backup solutions or Windows' built-in backup and recovery features can ensure easy recovery if something goes wrong during the upgrade process.

When clean installing Windows 11, it is recommended to create bootable USB installation media using the Installation Media Creation Tool. This allows installation from scratch, ideal for users preferring a new system configuration without residue from the previous installation. For example, formatting the hard drive and installing Windows 11 from the USB installation media ensures a clean and optimal installation of the operating system.

During the installation process, users are guided through steps such as selecting language, time zone, and configuration preferences. Once the installation is complete, it is recommended to check for available updates to ensure that Windows 11 is fully up to date with the latest security fixes and features. For example, accessing Windows Update settings after installation allows you to download and install necessary updates to improve system stability and security.

Finally, after upgrading to Windows 11, users can explore the new features like new Start menu, UI improvements, and optimized performance. It is advisable to explore settings and customization options to take full advantage of the new capabilities of the operating system. For example, setting up virtual desktops, customizing the theme, and exploring new pre-installed apps can enrich the user experience in Windows 11.

Data transfer and applications

Moving data and applications when migrating to a new IT environment, such as Windows 11, is a crucial step to ensure continuity and familiarity with the new operating system while preserving existing configurations. This process involves the efficient management of personal files, application settings and user data to minimize disruption and potential loss during the transition.

Firstly, it is recommended to backup all important data before starting the transfer process. Using external storage devices, cloud computing services, or local backup solutions can ensure the security of critical files. For example, copying documents, images, videos and other files to an external hard drive or to a cloud service like OneDrive or Google Drive ensures a backup before any changes.

Secondly, to transfer installed apps, it is better to check the compatibility of these apps with Windows 11. Some apps may require updates or may not be compatible with the new version of the operating system. In this case, it is recommended to download the most recent versions of applications from publisher websites or official application stores. For example, Microsoft's Office apps may require updating to the version compatible with Windows 11 to work properly.

Third, for users who prefer a more automated approach, specific migration tools can be used.

Windows offers built-in tools like the File and Settings Transfer Wizard, which make it easy to transfer user data, personalization settings, and even installed apps to a new computer or new installation of Windows 11. These tools can simplify the process by reducing the need for manual interventions and ensuring continuity of personalized settings.

Fourth, for specific apps that are not compatible with Windows 11 or for which no updates are available, it may be necessary to look for compatible alternatives. For example, if a third-party productivity app is not compatible with Windows 11, it may be beneficial to find an equivalent alternative that offers similar functionality while being compatible with the new operating system.

Fifth, after the data and applications are transferred, it is recommended to verify their integrity and operation on the new Windows 11 environment. Test the applications to ensure that they meet the user's needs and work correctly is essential to avoid any surprises or post-migration malfunctions. For example, opening important files in their associated applications and checking overall system stability after transfer can quickly identify potential issues.

Sixth, when transferring settings and personal configurations, it is helpful to document specific preferences before reconfiguring them on Windows 11. This includes desktop personalization settings, keyboard shortcuts, browser bookmarks, and other user preferences . Keeping a detailed list of custom adjustments can facilitate a smooth transition and reduce the time it takes to return to a familiar work environment.

Seventh, for more complex IT environments, involving multiple users or shared network configurations, advance planning and coordination are essential. In these cases, using IT asset management tools or professional migration solutions can simplify the process and reduce operational disruption. For example, businesses can use tools like Microsoft Endpoint Manager to manage the transfer of data and applications centrally and securely.

Finally, once the transfer of data and applications is complete, it is advisable to conduct a post-migration assessment to identify any remaining issues or necessary adjustments. Responding quickly to potential issues and providing adequate user support can improve users' overall Windows 11 experience. For example, providing additional training on new Windows 11 features or work environment-specific adjustments can maximize efficiency and user satisfaction after migration.

Conclusion

In conclusion, this Windows 11 book was designed to provide users, whether new or experienced, with a comprehensive and accessible resource for taking full advantage of Microsoft's new operating system. Through its many chapters, it explored in detail the essential aspects of Windows 11, from system requirements to advanced user interface customization, including installation, application management, and troubleshooting. common problems.

By going through this book, readers were able to gain an in-depth understanding of Windows 11's innovative features such as the new Start menu, virtual desktops, and expanded customization options. Additionally, they learned how to effectively navigate File Explorer, manage system settings, secure their device, and optimize performance for a smooth and secure user experience.

Additionally, this book focused on the importance of backing up data, moving apps and settings when migrating to Windows 11, offering practical tips and solutions to potential challenges encountered during this transition . It also covered advanced topics such as using recovery tools and managing system updates, ensuring that readers are prepared to efficiently troubleshoot problems and maintain the stability of their system.

Ultimately, this book aims to empower users by providing them with the knowledge and skills needed to fully exploit the capabilities of Windows 11 and to adapt to future technological developments. Whether for daily work, entertainment, or productivity, the information in this book is intended to enrich users' computing experience, allowing them to navigate the dynamic world of Windows 11 with confidence.